# PIER FISHING

**MINDY MOZER**

rosen publishing's
**rosen
central**®

New York

Published in 2014 by The Rosen Publishing Group, Inc.
29 East 21st Street, New York, NY 10010

**Library of Congress Cataloging-in-Publication Data**

Mozer, Mindy.
Pier fishing/Mindy Mozer.—1st ed.—New York: Rosen, c2014
    p. cm.—(Fishing: tips and techniques)
Includes bibliographical references and index.
ISBN: 978-1-4488-9488-8 (Library Binding)
ISBN: 978-1-4488-9506-9 (Paperback)
ISBN: 978-1-4488-9507-6 (6-pack)
1. Saltwater fishing. 2. Saltwater fishing—Juvenile literature. 3. Big game fishing. I. Title.
SH457 .M694 2014
799.16

*Manufactured in the United States of America*

CPSIA Compliance Information: Batch #S13YA: For further information, contact Rosen Publishing, New York,
New York, at 1-800-237-9932.

# CONTENTS

*E*leven-year-old Jaycob Rochelle caught a tarpon that was nearly twice his height at Surf City Pier in Surf City, North Carolina. The fish, which weighed 133.8 pounds (61 kilograms) and was 70 inches (1.8 meters) long, took two hours to reel in. The boy had set out that day to catch kingfish, a kind of fish that usually weighs closer to 30 pounds (14 kg). He didn't go out in a boat. He wasn't deep-sea fishing. He was fishing from a pier—a structure leading out from the shore into a body of water. In this case, the water was the Atlantic Ocean. He set a new fishing record for this particular pier, which is 937 feet (286 m) long with a 40-foot (12-m) octagon at the end. His fish beat the old record by more than 7 pounds (3 kg).

Fishing has long been a popular sport worldwide, and its popularity continues to grow. A recent National Survey of Fishing, Hunting, and Wildlife-Associated Recreation shows that 8.5 million six- to fifteen-year-olds in the United States fish. The number of anglers sixteen and older increased by 11 percent between 2006 and 2011. People have been fishing for almost as long as there have been what scientists consider modern human beings. Many records indicate that as long as forty thousand years

A man fishes in the ocean from a wooden pier—a structure leading out from the shore into a body of water. Fishermen on a pier can catch a variety of fish, depending on where the pier is located, the time of day, and the season.

ago, fishing was an important activity for humans, and fish were an important part of the human diet. Today, people fish for many reasons. For some, it is a way to put food on the table. For others, it is an excuse to spend a day outside surrounded by nature with family and friends. Still others like the sport of fishing—the thrill of pursuing and catching the big one.

Fishermen on a pier can catch a variety of fish, depending on where the pier is located and the time of day and year when they fish. It can also make a difference where they stand on the pier. Once fish are caught, anglers must clean and store them properly.

Whatever one's reason for fishing and one's desired catch, it's the responsibility of all anglers to practice basic safety techniques and good sportsmanship. This includes everything from water safety and having a fishing license to following legal guidelines for size requirements. A good fisherman is concerned about fishing's impact on the environment. This includes being aware of overfishing, knowing which fish should and should not be kept after being caught, and recognizing that a fisherman's actions have impacts on fish populations and on other fishermen.

With the right equipment, an understanding of the best fishing conditions, and attentiveness to safety and legal guidelines, anglers can be both successful and beneficial to the environment. Whether they are out to catch tomorrow's dinner or simply enjoy the calm of a weekend sunrise, they will find that fishing is an enjoyable pastime. You may not set new records when you cast or drop your line into the water, but you will be part of a long tradition in human history, one that you can help extend into future generations.

# CHAPTER 1

# FISHING SAFELY AND RESPONSIBLY

**B**efore making that first cast, there are important things to know about safety and sportsmanship. Even though anglers fishing from a pier are not in a boat on the water, they still need to be concerned about safety. This includes being aware of possible hazards, dressing appropriately, and paying attention to state regulations. There are also guidelines surrounding sportsmanship and fishing etiquette.

## Water Safety

Children under the age of thirteen should wear a life jacket. Each state has regulations regarding life jacket use. To work correctly, a life jacket must be snug. Children should never borrow an adult life jacket because it will be too big and not work properly. Life jackets should be tested for wear once a year. Leaky jackets should be thrown away. Adults and older teenagers who are strong swimmers and who do not want to wear a life jacket on a pier should bring with them a personal flotation device that can be thrown into the water. This device should be attached to 50 feet (15 m) of rope and can be thrown to someone who falls in the water.

The most important rule regarding water safety is to always have a buddy. Beginners especially can benefit from having a more experienced angler with them. If something does go wrong, there is someone close by to help or someone to call others for help. Finally, anglers should let others know where they are planning to fish. That way, if there's a

Pier fishermen can often enjoy a scenic view like this spot on Gould's Inlet, between St. Simons East Beach and the south tip of Sea Island in Georgia.

problem, others will know where to find them. It's a good idea to pack a fully charged cell phone with the rest of your gear.

# What to Wear

There's more to water safety than a life jacket. It's important for anglers to dress appropriately. Always wear shoes. This is especially true for fishermen on a pier because it can be wet. An angler doesn't want to fall while reeling in the big one. Bring a jacket. It might be cooler along the lake or ocean because of the breeze. A fisherman should also wear a hat, which protects from sunburn, and sunglasses, to protect the eyes from the sun. It's easy to get a sunburn standing so close to the water because the water reflects the sun's rays. Apply sunscreen, and remember insect repellent to keep mosquitoes and other biting insects away.

# Etiquette

Now that a fisherman is dressed appropriately and thinking about water safety, he or she has to be considerate of other anglers in the area, especially when fishing on a public pier. Public piers can get crowded. If fishermen don't act appropriately, someone could get hurt. Here are some guidelines:

- Never set up shop next to others fishing the area. Stay at least several feet away. If a person is not fishing, ask permission before throwing in a line. Do not walk in front of others who are fishing. Never fish in a swimming area. Also do not fish in areas that allow dogs.
- If you find a good fishing spot on the water, you should fish there for a while and then move on so that others can enjoy the area. Also be careful not to fish too closely to friends. Lines can get tangled.

Fishermen need to be considerate of others, especially when fishing on a public pier. A good guideline is to stay several feet away from others fishing, so lines don't get tangled.

• Never throw a line over or between fishermen. Don't cast over someone fighting a fish. If a person is reeling in a fish, he or she may need to enter another fisherman's space. That is acceptable. Be polite—offer to take a picture.

• If fishing in a private pond, be sure to get permission from the landowner first. If an angler doesn't do so, he or she is considered to be trespassing.

• You should clean up before you leave. Carry all litter out. Throw away trash in garbage cans and put unused bait in the water. Never throw trash into the water.

# Hazards of Mercury

Seafood has many health benefits. It is low in fat and contains protein. Salmon has omega-3 acids, which help prevent heart disease. But fish eaters should be aware that small amounts of mercury can be found in almost all fish and shellfish. Mercury is a poisonous metal that could harm the developing nervous system of a young child or unborn baby. Mercury is released into the air from factories and then enters lakes and oceans. Bacteria in the water chemically alter the mercury, creating a substance called methylmercury. Small fish eat the methylmercury. Then bigger fish eat the small fish. That's why the biggest fish, such as sharks, have the highest levels of mercury.

For most people, the risks of mercury from eating fish or shellfish are not a concern. The Food and Drug Administration (FDA) and the Environmental Protection Agency (EPA) recommend that women who may become pregnant, are pregnant, or are nursing mothers should avoid fish high in mercury. The agencies also say young children should not eat fish high in mercury. Here are some guidelines outlined by these agencies for people at risk:

- Avoid eating the biggest fish with the highest levels of mercury, such as shark, swordfish, or king mackerel.
- Eat no more than two meals a week of fish or shellfish. Fish low in mercury are shrimp, canned light tuna, salmon, and catfish.
- See if there are local health advisories about the fish in local lakes and rivers. If there are, do not eat those fish. If there are not any advisories, eat only one meal of fish caught from local waters a week.

• You should release all fish back into the lake or ocean that aren't wanted. You should be careful about overfishing with multiple rods at a time. Use two rods at the most, and put other rods away so that they aren't in the way.

• Finally, you should share with those nearby. If a neighbor runs out of something, such as bait, offer him or her some of yours.

# Equipment Safety

In the reservoirs of the Illinois River, Asian carp jump from the river when boats approach. They have even been known to hit fishermen in

Anglers should carry fishing rods parallel to the ground and remove fishing hooks before transporting them.

the face. Although this isn't likely to happen when pier fishing, there are safety considerations to be aware of when handling equipment.

The biggest safety hazard comes from fishing hooks. Anglers should carry their rods parallel to the ground and remove fishing hooks before transporting them. Hooks on rods that aren't being used should have a safety cover. A fishing hook is made up of different parts. A hook's point is the part that catches the fish. It is sharp and can hurt an angler if he or she accidentally gets hooked. The eye of the hook connects the hook to the fishing line or lure. The shank of the hook connects the eye and hook. When touching a hook, hold the shank.

Fishermen should also use caution when using fishing line. It is easy to get tangled if a fisherman isn't paying attention. When casting, you should make sure no one is behind you. Otherwise, you could hit someone in the face or body. Fishing knives can also cause injuries if fishermen aren't careful. Never hold a knife by its blade, and, when storing it, put it into a protective case.

# State and Federal Regulations

Being a responsible fisherman means honoring state and federal regulations regarding fishing. The laws are designed to protect fish and to make sure everyone has an equal chance to enjoy the sport. The first rule is to buy required licenses.

Fishermen need a license to fish. Each state has different rules and regulations regarding fishing licenses. The money raised from fishing licenses helps pay for fishery and hatchery management, habitat development, and fishing and conservation education. Most states require residents to be at least sixteen years old to get a license. The license is good for one year. A license may not be needed when fishing in a private pond, depending on the state. Most states require residents to show proof that they live in the state, such as a driver's license.

FISHING LICENSE REQUIRED

CAUTION!
ALLIGATORS
NO SWIMMING

WE ARE CONCERNED ABOUT PEOPLE

WE ARE CONCERNED ABOUT WILDLIFE
Florida Department

This small Florida freshwater fishing pond in Topsail Hill Preserve State Park reminds visitors that a fishing license is required.

Check state laws when trying to determine if children under the age of sixteen need a fishing license. Some states require children to fish with a licensed adult. Also check for rules regarding nonresident licenses. Some states offer short-term licenses to accommodate vacationers. Fishing licenses can be purchased from county clerks, at sporting goods stores, or online, depending on the state.

Be sure to honor catch limits, which can vary from state to state and are in force to protect the fish population. It also is against the law to catch certain types of fish when they aren't in season. If fishermen see others breaking the law, they should report them. It's up to everyone to protect the fish population. Overfishing will ruin the sport for everyone and endanger its future.

# CHAPTER 2

## GEARING UP

A pier fisherman doesn't have to spend a fortune on fishing equipment to be successful. Here is a look at the different types of equipment and what each piece does.

## Fishing Rods

A fishing rod is the key piece of equipment for any fisherman. There is a difference between a fishing rod and a fishing pole. A fishing rod has guides and a reel. Guides are the rings on the rod that guide the line from the reel, down the rod, to the tip. They are metal or ceramic. A reel winds and unwinds fishing line. A fishing pole has no guides and no reel. Instead, the line is simply attached to the tip at a fixed length. It cannot be reeled in or out but simply dropped into the water and jerked out.

Rods are made out of different materials. The earliest fishing rods

A fishing rod has guides and a reel. Guides are the rings on the rod that guide the line from the reel, down the rod, to the tip. A reel winds and unwinds fishing line.

were made from tree limbs or cane stalks. Today, they are made of fiberglass or graphite. Rods are sold in different lengths. Some come in one piece, while others are two-piece rods, which are easier to carry. Here are the parts of a rod:

- **Butt:** The thickest part of the rod closest to the handle.
- **Butt cap:** This is at the bottom of the handle.
- **Handle:** Where a fisherman holds the rod. Most handles are made of foam or cork.
- **Reel seat:** Where the reel is attached to the rod.
- **Windings:** How the guides are attached to a rod.

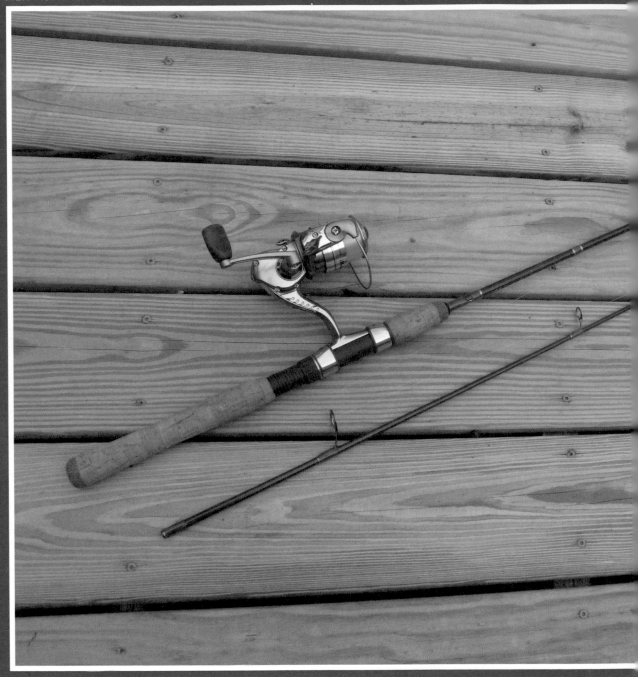

Fishing rods are sold in different lengths. Some come in one piece, while others are two-piece rods, which are easier to carry.

• **Ferrule:** The part that joins together the two halves of a two-piece rod.

The type of rod a fisherman should use depends on the type of fishing he or she wishes to do. There are different types of rods. Pier fishermen need a rod that is big enough to handle fish up to 20 pounds (9 kg). Any of the following rods can be used for pier fishing:

• **Casting:** Casting rods are used with lures or bait for light bottom fishing.
• **Spinning:** Spinning rods are like casting rods but use a spinning reel. A spinning fishing rod has big guides, which the fishing line passes through.
• **Surf rods:** They are from 9 feet to 14 feet (3–4 m) long and are designed for long casts to launch the bait out and away from the beach.

When purchasing a rod, there are some things to think about. These considerations include:

• **Length:** The length of a rod will usually determine how far a pier fisherman can cast. Longer rods are better for lure casting. Shorter rods usually have heavier fishing line and are better for bottom fishing. Pay attention to the weight of a rod. A fisherman can get tired using a heavy rod. Also anglers should consider where they will be fishing. If they will be walking or driving to their favorite fishing spot, they should get a rod that breaks down in at least two sections so that it is easier to carry.

• **Guides:** Guides come in different forms. Ceramic guides cost more but allow longer casts. Roller guides are used on bottom fishing rigs. Stainless-steel guides are used for wire line applications. Standard metal guides cost less and are good for bottom fishing.

• **Taper:** The amount of bend a rod has, which is measured from slow to extra fast. A slow taper makes it difficult to cast heavy bait. A fast taper will bend in the upper section of the rod. A rod with an extra-fast taper usually costs more but can engage with bigger fish.

# Fishing Line

Fishing line is the string connecting the rod and reel to the lure. Early fishermen used pieces of twine as line. By the Middle Ages, braided horsehair was used as fishing line. Some deep-sea fishermen twisted linen into fishing line.

Most fishing line today is made out of nylon in a single-strand, which is called monofilament. The other type of fishing line is braided. This is line made from multiple fibers braided together. A single line sinks faster than a braided line. Fishing lines come in different sizes, colors, and line strengths. Brown or red lines, for example, are sometimes used by fishermen in muddy waters so that the lines are camouflaged.

# Hooks

A fishing hook is what catches the fish. The type of fishing hook to use depends on the type of fish a person wants to catch. Here are things

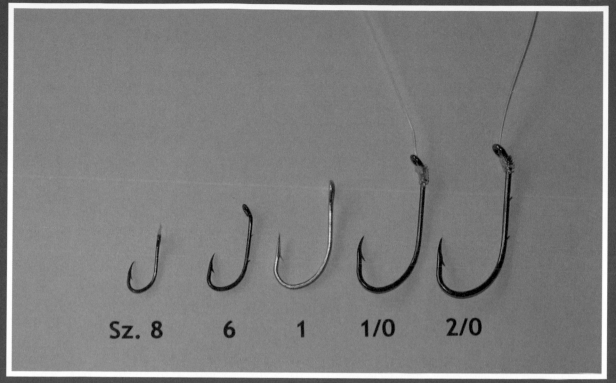

Sz. 8    6    1    1/0    2/0

Hooks come in different sizes. Hooks are classified by number. The higher the number, the smaller the hook.

to think about when picking out a hook. Larger hooks are used to catch bigger fish. A hook needs to be big enough to hold both the bait and the fish. But if it's too large, a fish will detect it. Hooks are classified by number, but a large number doesn't mean a large hook. Instead, the higher the number, the smaller the hook. A twenty hook is smaller than a ten hook, for example.

Fishermen who plan to catch and release fish back into the lake or ocean often use hooks with a barbless point so that the fish aren't harmed. A barb is the sharp part that sticks out near the end of the hook.

# Bait

Picking the perfect bait is key to having a successful pier fishing trip. Bait is what fishermen use to attract fish. Fish are attracted to motion, sound, smell, touch, and taste. Fish recognize when an object, such as a plastic worm tail, is moving. They pick up vibrations. Some odors also attract fish. Bait appeals to these senses. For example, a fish is attracted by sight to a colorful plastic worm and by sound to the worm brushing against a lake bottom.

A popular live bait is the earthworm. Worms are sold at bait shops or general fishing stores. Some serious fishermen raise their own worms. Other types of live bait are minnows, crickets, and grasshoppers. Fishermen fishing in salt water might use bunkers, snappers, shrimp, or herring as live bait.

Fishermen can also use fishing lure. Lures come in different sizes and colors. Some are made to resemble worms, crawfish, or other types of natural bait. Jigs are a common type of lure. They have a tail that is made of animal hair, feathers, or plastic and a metal head. They can be used to catch both freshwater and saltwater fish. Spoons are flat metal lures that look like the bottom of a spoon with a hook. Plugs, which are made of plastic or wood, are used on top of the water and resemble baitfish. Spinners have blades that twist and make noise. Plastic worms and minnows can be bought in various colors and sizes. Poppers and flies are used with fly fishing.

# Sinkers and Weights

Sinkers are generally used with live-bait fishing, while weights are used with artificial lures. They are both made of lead or steel. Their job is to make sure the hook sinks so that the bait is on the bottom of the lake or ocean. They are pinched onto the line or slide onto the line. Sinkers

# Top 10 Things You Should Have in Your Tackle Box

1. **Extra line:** If your fishing line breaks or gets tangled, your fishing trip can continue if you have extra line.

2. **Extra hooks:** You don't know how big the fish will be until you catch one. Make sure you bring hooks of different sizes so that you are ready for anything.

3. **Extra lures:** Bring extra lures in case you lose one while fishing.

4. **Bobbers and sinkers:** Carry an assortment of bobbers and sinkers. Bobbers keep bait floating. Sinkers help bait sink to the bottom.

5. **Plastic worms:** In case you run out of bait.

6. **Pliers:** Have pliers ready if you need to cut a line or replace hooks.

7. **First-aid kit:** Make sure you have bandages and antiseptic for minor cuts. It's easy to cut yourself with a hook.

8. **Sunscreen:** A sunburn can ruin a beautiful day. Be sure to protect your skin.

9. **Flashlight:** In case you lose track of time and it gets dark.

10. **Duct tape:** This will come in handy if your fishing rod breaks.

come in different sizes and different weights. In deep water, fishermen use a heavier sinker.

## Floats or Bobbers

Floats, which are also called bobbers, are the opposite of sinkers and weights. They keep bait from sinking. They come in different colors and

Fishermen who do not want to use live bait can use fishing lures. Lures come in different sizes and colors, and some resemble natural bait.

shapes. Some even glow in the dark. A bobber indicates that a fish has been caught by moving down. A fish bites, and the float jiggles and then goes below the surface. The size and shape of the float used depends on the weight of the bait, the water current, and wind conditions.

# Gaff, Pliers, and Scissors

A gaff is used to pull the fish onto the shore, especially when the fish weighs more than the fishing line can support. A gaff, which is a pole with a sharp hook on the end, is important if the fish has sharp teeth. Fishermen use a gaff to bring a fish out of the water.

Fishermen should remember to bring something to remove the hook from a fish's mouth. Pliers work best. A fisherman should never use his or her bare hands to remove hooks. Also be sure to pack a good pair of scissors that are strong enough to snip fishing line.

# CHAPTER 3

# PIER FISHING BASICS

A pier is a walkway above a body of water. Think of a pier as a bridge that doesn't go anywhere. Some piers are so big that restaurants and shopping centers are built on them. One of the longest piers in the United States is the Santa Cruz Wharf in California. The wharf is 2,701 feet (823 m) long and is about 22 feet (7 m) above the tide. The wharf was built by the city of Santa Cruz in 1914. Today, it features restaurants and gift shops. Fishing is also a popular activity on the wharf.

Another long pier is the Skyway Fishing Pier State Park in Florida. The pier was created after a new bridge was built over Tampa Bay along the Gulf of Mexico to connect St. Petersburg with Palmetto. Since the old bridge was no longer needed, it was turned into a public fishing pier. The pier provides more than 4 miles (6.4 km) of fishing space. It is lit up at night, and this light attracts fish.

The advantage of fishing from a pier is that fishermen are able to reach deeper

One of the longest piers in the United States is the Santa Cruz Wharf in California. The wharf features restaurants, gift shops, and plenty of pier fishing.

sections of the lake or ocean below them without requiring access to a boat. The type of fish they catch, the techniques they use, and the methods of reeling in fish vary depending on the type of water in which they are fishing.

# In the Ocean

When a fisherman fishes in the ocean, it is called saltwater fishing. This is because oceans are filled with salt water. A variety of fish can be caught from an ocean pier. Florida fishing guidebooks, for example, note that, in January, redfish and flounder are popular catches. By July, the list includes bluefish, Spanish mackerel, and lady fish. This shift is caused by migration.

Migration is the movement of fish from one place to another. Fish migrate to feed and to breed. Some fish migrate from large areas of water, such as the ocean, to rivers. This is called anadromous migration. Salmon and sturgeon engage in anadromous migration. When fish migrate from the river to the ocean, it is called catadromous migration. Eels engage in catadromous migration. Other species of fish may migrate from a deeper area to a more shallow area within the same body of water where they can then spawn, or deposit eggs.

On long piers, such as the Santa Cruz Wharf, there are many different types of fish that can be caught because the pier reaches different parts of the ocean. Along the beach, anglers typically catch calico surfperch. Midway out on the pier, fishermen catch kingfish, walleye surfperch, silver surfperch, white seaperch, and shinerperch that swim above the sandy bottom. Debris typically builds up at the farthest ocean end of the pier, forming an artificial reef. Fishermen here can catch a variety of fish, including salmon. On the Skyway Fishing Pier State Park in Florida, fishermen catch snook, tarpon, grouper, black sea bass, Spanish mackerel, king mackerel, cobia, sheepshead, red snapper, and pompano.

This bucket is full of walleye, which are large predatory fish. They tend to feed at dawn, dusk, and on cloudy or choppy days, and these are the best times to catch them.

Here are some general guidelines on where to catch fish from an ocean pier:

• Bluefish are often near moving water and travel in schools. Look for birds diving into the water. The birds are eating baitfish that bluefish also like to eat.

• Croaker come near shore to feed when the water is murky, so they can be caught on calm days from the beach end of a pier.

• Flounder can be found in clear, calm water. They like to feed in moving water—high tide or low tide. To catch them, you should fish near jetties, points, and the inside edges of sandbars.

- King mackerel can be found in shallow water. They feed in moderate surf.
- Red drum stay farther out but will come closer in to feed. They feed in rough water and probably won't bite on calm days.
- Spanish mackerel are caught in warm, clear water. Diving birds are a sign that these fish are nearby.
- Spot are good fish to catch from a pier. They are named spot because they have a spot behind their gills. They are commonly caught in the surf.
- Sheepshead are also good to catch from a pier because they feed near structures.

# In Lakes and Ponds

Piers can also be found over lakes, where freshwater fish live. Freshwater fish like to hide in plants, and these plants grow under and near piers. Plants attract small fish, and small fish, in turn, attract big fish. Piers also protect fish from the sun. The combination of these factors makes a pier the perfect spot for freshwater fishing.

Largemouth bass are one of the most popular types of fish to catch in lakes and ponds. They are dark green or olive with greenish-yellowish sides. They have a dark stripe down the side of the body. They can be found in groups around trees, large rocks, and underwater dock pilings. They eat smaller fish, frogs, crayfish, and insects. Largemouth bass grow 4 to 6 inches (10 to 15 cm) during their first year and can get to 16 inches (41 cm) in three years. The average size of a largemouth bass is 3 to 10 pounds (1 to 4.5 kg), but the fish can grow up to 20 pounds (9 kg) in some cases. Smallmouth bass are also popular fish in lakes and ponds. Smallmouth bass like rocks and sand or gravel bottoms. They like cooler and clearer water than largemouth bass. The average smallmouth bass is 3 pounds (1 kg) but can grow up to 12 pounds (5.5 kg).

A hooked walleye is hauled in. In some regions, walleye are also known as pickerel, colored pike, or yellow pike.

In addition, fishermen can catch fish from the pike family in lakes and ponds. The muskellunge, or the muskie, is the biggest member of the pike family. Other members include the northern pike and the pickerel. Panfish are the smallest fish in lakes and ponds. They include bluegills, crappies, rock bass, sunfish, and yellow perch. Trout can also be found in lakes and ponds, although they prefer streams. Rainbow trout are a popular game fish for fly fishermen. Rainbow trout like cold water rivers and streams.

## Other Factors to Consider

The best time to fish is when the fish are feeding. That is typically at dusk and dawn. The crowds haven't gathered yet on the pier in the early morning, so there isn't as much competition. Experienced fishermen say it's best to arrive just before the sun comes up. The same is true at sunset. Arrive thirty minutes before the sun goes down. After sundown, the pier may again be crowded with people.

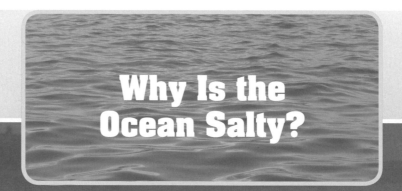

# Why Is the Ocean Salty?

Salt in the ocean actually comes from inland water sources. Water flowing in rivers carries small amounts of mineral salts from the rocks and soil of the riverbeds. The river water makes its way to oceans, increasing the sea's salinity. The sun evaporates ocean water, but the salt is left behind.

Time of day can determine one's success with the rod and reel, but so, too, can weather, which can make the difference between a good fishing trip and a bad fishing trip. Fish can sense the weather and are able to detect pressure changes. Some weather factors to consider when pier fishing:

- **Temperature:** When fishing in freshwater, dawn and dusk tend to be the best times because it is cooler and the fish are actively feeding. When it is hot outside, fish stay in deeper water to cool off. So on hot days, a fisherman should use top water lures and bait

Weather can make the difference between a good fishing trip and a bad fishing trip. Rain causes organic matter to be washed into the water, luring fish to the surface to eat.

during the coolest part of the day—early morning or late in the day. During the midday hours, use deep fishing baits and lures.

- **Wind:** If it is a windy day, cast into the wind from the shore.
- **Storms:** Fish are attuned to changes in weather patterns. Fish may eat more right before a cold front passes through but eat less during and after a storm or front's passage. The high pressure that comes with cold fronts also makes fish slower and discourages them from coming near the surface of the water. That's why fishing during and right after the arrival of a cold front isn't the best time. However, warm fronts make fish more interested in eating, especially in the warm part of the water. Lower pressure will bring fish closer to the surface.
- **Clouds:** Fish like to eat on cloudy days rather than on bright days.
- **Rain:** Rain causes insects to fly near the surface of the water, which attracts fish to the surface and makes it easier for them to be caught. Rain also causes organic matter to be washed into the water, luring fish to the surface to eat. During heavy rain showers, however, fish can have a hard time seeing bait.
- **Tides:** If fishing on the ocean, pay attention to the tides. A prime fishing spot during a high tide can be too shallow during low tides. A good low tide spot might have too much water depth during high tides. Some say the best time to fish is during the transition from high to low tides.

# CHAPTER 4

# AFTER THE CATCH

Fish are not only fun to catch, but they are good to eat. They are a healthy protein choice, rich in vitamins and minerals, low in saturated fat, and lower in calories than a similar portion of meat or poultry. Some fish, such as salmon and mackerel, are high in omega-3 fatty acids. That is a type of fat that helps make a person's blood less likely to form clots that can cause heart attacks. But before a fish can be eaten, a fisherman first has to reel a fish in, keep the fish cool and fresh, prepare the fish for cooking, and cook it properly.

## Reeling in a Fish

The most important thing to remember when reeling in a fish is to stay calm. Keep pressure on the line. This helps control the fish as it moves through the water and keeps the hook from breaking. When the fish is fighting hard, stop reeling it in. That way, the line doesn't break.

Fish need to be taken care of immediately after they are caught so that they don't spoil. A good method is to put fish on ice.

Raise the tip of the fishing pole so that it stays up, but hold the reel at eye level. A fisherman should keep his or her body facing the direction of the fish and move around the pier if necessary. Fishermen should reel the fish in until they can grab it with a net. If the fish is small, a net might not be needed.

## Immediate Storage

Once caught, fish need to be properly taken care of so that they don't spoil. Fish need to be kept fresh from the moment they come out of the water until they are fully cooked. The best method to keep a fish fresh

# Mounting a Fish

Instead of eating a fish, some people like to mount it for display in their home. Mounting an animal is considered by some to be an art form because it takes a lot of work to make the fish look lifelike. Taxidermy professionals, or the people who mount animals, say a fish is particularly challenging to mount because they have to make it appear to be in its natural element and in fluid motion.

is to put it on ice. Fishermen have to plan ahead and bring an insulated cooler with a lot of ice. Make sure the cooler's drain plug is open so that the melt water runs out. Water can spoil the flavor of the fish. Put the fish on top of the ice or pack ice around them.

Before preparing the fish to eat, check the fish for signs of disease. A healthy fish should have bright clear eyes, red gills, and firm flesh with no signs of browning. A diseased fish may have sunken eyes, discolored skin, open wounds, or gills that are white and slimy.

## Cleaning Fish

Once the fish are brought home, it's time to clean them. Here are some cleaning techniques:

1. **Dressing:** This is cleaning the fish. When dressing a fish, the fisherman removes the guts, head, and fins.
2. **Scaling:** This is when the scales are removed from the skin of the fish. It is usually done before a fish is dressed.

3. **Skinning:** This is when the skin is removed from the entire fish. This is also done before a fish is dressed.

4. **Filleting:** These are pieces of meat that do not have bones or skin, like the fillets sold in a supermarket. Filleting means removing the meat from the sides of the fish so that there are no bones.

5. **Steaking:** This is when the fish is cut into steaks. This technique is primarily used with large fish. At the grocery store, people can often buy salmon or tuna steaks. A steaked fish is first scaled or skinned and then dressed.

The bones and skin of the fish are removed to make fillets like those sold in the supermarket. This is known as "cleaning" the fish.

# Storing Fish

How a person stores fish after it has been cleaned depends on when he or she plans to eat it. If you plan to cook the fish in a day or two, pat down the fish with a kitchen towel to remove excess moisture and place the fish in a bag or container. Place the container in the refrigerator or in an insulated cooler filled with ice. Never let the fish come in contact with the water because it will spoil the taste.

If you plan to use the fish more than two days after catching it, it is best to freeze it. Fish can last for several months in the freezer. Pat down the fish with a kitchen towel to remove moisture and place the fish in plastic wrap or aluminum foil. Then put the fish in a layer of freezer paper. Or place the fish in plastic containers, fill with water, cover, and freeze. To thaw the frozen fish, put it in cold water or in the refrigerator. Thawed fish should be used within one or two days. Keep raw fish and cooked fish separate.

# Cooking and Eating Fish

It is important to handle seafood safely to reduce the risk of food poisoning. This starts with keeping raw fish and cooked fish separate. It's best to cook seafood to reduce the chance of foodborne illness. If a person chooses to eat raw fish, one suggestion is to eat fish that has been previously frozen. Some species of fish can contain parasites, and freezing can kill these harmful microorganisms. But freezing won't kill all parasites, so it's best to cook seafood. Some people have a greater risk for foodborne illness and should stay away from raw or partially cooked fish or shellfish. Those people include pregnant women, young children, older adults, and people whose immune systems are weak.

Fish is done cooking when the flesh turns opaque and begins to flake easily when tested with a fork. Be careful not to overcook fish.

Fish is done cooking when the flesh turns opaque and begins to flake easily when tested with a fork. Undercooked fish can be dangerous to your health, and overcooked fish can be dry, rubbery, and stinky.

Overcooked fish becomes tough and often has a bad flavor. Cooking times vary with the type and size of fish.

Be careful when eating fish not to choke on small bones. Some fish, such as panfish and trout, are filled with small bones. When cleaning the fish, it can be hard to remove every bone.

# Catch-and-Release

Not every fisherman catches fish for food. For those who fish purely for recreation, there's catch-and-release. In some areas, only catch-and-release fishing is allowed. Other areas may have minimum size regulations. If a fisherman catches a fish that is too small, it has to be released. Catch-and-release is also used after fishermen have caught their legal limit of fish. Here are some catch-and-release guidelines:

- Use single hooks. Single hooks are faster and easier to remove. Pinch the barb on the hook to make releasing the fish easier.
- Decide if you are going to release a fish before it is caught and definitely before it is taken out of the water.

Some fishermen prefer to release fish. A good guideline for catch-and-release fishing is to use single hooks, which are faster and easier to remove.

- When retrieving a hooked fish, stay steady. Don't pull the fish up too quickly, which will cause extra stress, or too slowly, which will physically exhaust the fish.
- Use needle-nosed pliers to pry the hook from the fish while it is still in the water. If live bait or a lure is too deep in the fish's gullet to get out, cut the leader—the short length of line used to attach the end of the fishing line to the lure or hook—close to the fish's mouth, and let the fish keep the hook. Studies show fish can get rid of the hook on their own.
- Minimize how much time the fish stays out of water.
- Keep your hands moistened. This helps prevent removal of the fish's natural protective mucous layer and reduces the chance of future infections in the fish's skin.
- Return the fish to water headfirst.

Even if you don't keep the fish, that doesn't mean you can't share the catch with your family and friends. This is where a camera comes in handy. Take a picture of your amazing catch before carefully releasing it back into the water. In addition, a lot of taxidermists create fiberglass replicas of caught fish based on photographs taken before the fish is released back to the water. You can have your trophy and the gratification of knowing you've done something to ensure the future health of fish stocks and ocean life. It's the ultimate win-win!

# CHAPTER 5

## ENSURING THE FUTURE OF FISHING

*f*ishing is more than just a fun and pleasurable activity for many people around the world. Of every five people in the world, one of them depends on fish as his or her primary source of protein. Fish are an especially important part of the livelihood of people living in developing countries. But there's a worldwide concern that people are catching and eating fish faster than they can reproduce and replace themselves. This is called overfishing.

Overfishing is not a new problem. In the early 1800s, humans destroyed the whale population because they wanted blubber for lamp oil. By the mid-1900s, Atlantic cod and herring were overharvested. Today, there are serious worries about overfishing both by people who fish for recreation and those who fish for business (commercial fishermen).

According to the International Union for Conservation of Nature's Red List of endangered species, 5 percent

A fisherman separates a rockfish from the pile of menhaden. Fishermen are required to tag each rockfish they catch to help prevent the overfishing of them.

of the world's known species of fish are at risk of extinction. Habitat loss and pollution contribute to this danger, but the biggest threat is overfishing. The fish most at risk are large fish that are slow to reproduce. Of the 307 shark species, 50 are listed as vulnerable, endangered, or critically endangered. Some species of rockfish that can live to be over one hundred years old are depleted because of overfishing.

The number of endangered and threatened species in the United States changes as species are added and removed from the list. Below is a list of some of the world's most endangered fish. If a fisherman catches one of these fish, the best thing to do is release it back into the water. It is also helpful to write down where the fish was caught, if the fish was fully grown, and how many other fish were nearby. This information should be provided to local wildlife officials for record-keeping and research purposes.

### 1. Atlantic Halibut

Atlantic halibut can live for fifty years. A halibut can reach 9 feet (2.7 m) and weigh up to 1,000 pounds (454 kg). But it's at risk of extinction because it doesn't mature and reproduce until it is ten to fourteen years old.

## 2. Beluga Sturgeon

Beluga sturgeon are overfished because of their eggs, which are called caviar and are considered to be a delicacy. These fish can grow up to 15 feet (4.5 m), weigh more than a ton (907 kg), and live to be one hundred years old. Beluga sturgeon don't reach maturity until they are twenty or twenty-five years old.

## 3. Acadian Redfish

This North Atlantic fish can live as long as fifty years and grow to 20 inches (0.5 m). It reaches maturity at eight or nine years old. This fish is a victim of trawling. This is a fishing method in which a large fishing net is dragged behind a boat with the goal of catching a large quantity and variety of fish in one fell swoop.

## 4. Orange Roughy

Orange roughy live up to 149 years. This fish reaches maturity between twenty and thirty-two years. Orange roughy have been victims of fishermen trawling when the fish are feeding and breeding. This affects several generations of the fish simultaneously.

## 5. Winter Skate

This fish is harvested and processed into fishmeal and lobster bait. It is found in the northwest Atlantic Ocean. Winter skate are also victims of trawling. Their population numbers have fallen, some experts say by 90 percent since the 1970s, because they have few offspring.

## 6. Bocaccio Rockfish

Bocaccio rockfish are one of the more than seventy species of rockfish living off the West Coast of the United States. This 3-foot (1 m) fish reaches reproductive age as early as four or five. But it's endangered because its larvae have a low survival rate. Bocaccio larvae live long enough to become juveniles only once every twenty years.

### 7. European Eel
European eel are born at sea and then migrate to freshwater streams. They reach maturity at anywhere from six to thirty years in the freshwater streams and then return to sea to spawn. If they can't make it back to sea, they live in freshwater and can live for fifty years. If they make it back to salt water and reproduce, they die. Many of the European eels caught by fishermen at sea are juveniles that haven't had a chance to spawn.

### 8. Goliath Grouper
The Goliath grouper is a large fish that can grow to 7 feet (2 m) and live for forty years. It is threatened because it reproduces for a short period of time, resulting in fewer offspring.

### 9. Maltese Ray
The Maltese ray can be found in the Strait of Sicily, a channel between Italy and Tunisia. It grows slowly, matures late, and produces few offspring.

### 10. Bluefin Tuna
Bluefin tuna are found in the northern Atlantic Ocean. They can grow to 10 feet (3 m) and weigh more than 1,400 pounds (635 kg). This fish sells for a lot of money. As a result, it has been overfished by commercial fishermen.

# Regulations

The U.S. Fish and Wildlife Service works with state agencies to manage and set regulations on the amount of fish that can be caught, the type of fish that can be caught, and even what kind of fishing equipment that can

Bluefin tuna sells for a lot of money. For this reason, it has been overfished by commercial fishermen and its population is now under great stress.

be used by both commercial fishermen and recreational fishermen. These regulations can vary by state. In Louisiana, for example, the rules set out by the state's department of wildlife and fisheries vary by lake. In one lake, only eight largemouth bass are allowed to be caught in a day. States also set fishing seasons for various types of fish. In Minnesota, summer angling restrictions at one lake say that all northern pike 26 to 44 inches (0.7 to 1.1 m) must be immediately released. Those who violate these regulations risk being fined, having their fishing licenses revoked, and even getting arrested and charged with a crime.

# Responsible Fish Eating

One way individuals can help prevent the decline of fish populations is to be responsible fish eaters. This means choosing seafood that is caught or farmed in a way that minimizes harm to the ocean and the environment. Organizations that monitor the fish population have put together a guide called *The Fish List*. The list divides fish and shellfish into three categories: Go-Go Fish, So-So Fish, and No-No fish.

Go-Go Fish are the best choice. They are fast-growing species whose populations are doing well. Some fish are on this list because they are being successfully raised, or farmed, in large fish tanks and then sold to fish markets.

No-No Fish are fish that should not be eaten because they are either severely overfished or are harvested by methods that are destructive to other species or to water quality. Some species are on the do-not-eat list because they are slow-growing and do not reproduce at a rate that can replace population losses. Also found on this list are species that are plentiful but are farmed in ways that are harmful to the environment.

So-So Fish are in the middle. These fish are at risk of declining population or are fished in ways that impact their habitats, but not to the same degree of severity as the No-No fish (at least not yet).

Plastic bags and other trash and debris that are tossed into the ocean can choke, strangle, and sicken fish and other marine life. For the sake of ocean health, all trash must be carefully disposed of in the proper secure receptacles.

# Other Ways to Help

There are things people can do to help the fish population, and fishermen are uniquely well-positioned to make the most positive and impactful contribution to the health of freshwater and ocean fisheries.

- **Don't litter:** Plastic found in the oceans hurts marine life. A floating plastic bag looks like a jellyfish to sea turtles, for example. To seabirds, plastic pellets—the pieces that make up plastic products—look like fish eggs. Plastic can float on the surface for years because it is so durable. Individuals can help with this problem by throwing away all trash into designated trash receptacles, not into the water or along the shore.

# Disaster in the Gulf

In 2010, an explosion at an offshore drilling site owned by an oil and gas company called British Petroleum (BP) caused oil to spill into the Gulf of Mexico. For three months, oil gushed into the ocean. The spill caused beaches and marshes from Louisiana to Florida to be contaminated. The extent of the environmental damage is still unknown, but scientists suspect that fish were negatively affected and severely impacted by the petroleum. After the spill, fishermen reported catching grouper and red snapper with large open sores and strange black streaks they had never seen before. Because oil takes so long to break down, the spill will continue to affect the health of Gulf marine life—and perhaps the humans who consume the fish—for several generations at least.

- **Balloons:** Don't release balloons into the air. Many end up in the ocean, and marine life mistake them for food. They can then choke or sicken animals when they ingest balloon fragments.
- **Cut plastic six-pack holders:** If a six-pack can holder makes its way into the ocean, fish can get caught in them. Snip the holders before throwing them away into a designated trash receptacle.
- **Reuse and recycle:** This includes bringing reusable grocery bags when shopping.
- **No dumping:** Never pour paint, car fluids, and other liquids down storm drains or into bodies of water. These fluids may end up in lakes, streams, rivers, and oceans.
- **Local cleanups:** Whether it's cleaning up a neighborhood or the local waterway, take part in local cleanup days.

- **Pick up trash:** People shouldn't wait for a cleanup day to throw away littered trash. Set a good example and throw away littered cans, food wrappers, and other discarded waste.

# Pollution and the Ocean

Pollution is when harmful contaminants are introduced into an ecosystem. In the ocean, common pollutants include pesticides, herbicides, chemical fertilizers, detergents, oil, sewage, and plastics. For example, excess nutrients from fertilizer can produce algae. This

Don't wait for a cleanup day to pick up and properly dispose of littered trash (even if it isn't yours). Set a good example by collecting discarded cans, food wrappers, and other discarded waste every time you visit the shore.

creates an area where marine life can't exist. Marine mammals, fish, and birds may eat waste, such as plastic bags, thinking it is food. Old fishing nets that are thrown into the ocean can ensnare fish and mammals. An area in the North Pacific is called the trash vortex because it is full of decomposing plastic items and trash. The area is said to be as big as the state of Texas.

To ensure the future of the sport you love, and to be able to share and hand it down to your children, do everything you can to preserve the health of fish populations and their habitats. The future of fishing depends on you.

# GLOSSARY

**anadromous** Traveling up rivers from the sea to breed in freshwater.

**bait** Food used to attract fish. Bait can be live or artificial.

**catadromous** Living in freshwater but migrating to marine waters to breed.

**dressing** The process of cleaning fish. When dressing a fish, a fisherman removes the guts, head, and fins.

**endangered** At grave and imminent risk of extinction.

**filleting** Removing the meat from the sides of the fish so that there are no bones.

**fishing line** The string connecting the rod and reel to the lure.

**fishing pole** A fishing pole has no guides and no reel. Instead, the line is attached directly to the tip of the pole.

**fishing rod** A fishing rod has guides and a reel. Guides are the rings on the rod that guide the line down the rod, from the reel to the tip. A reel winds and unwinds fishing line.

**float** A device, also called a bobber, that keeps bait from sinking.

**gaff** A stick with a hook used for landing a fish.

**hook** The piece of fishing equipment that catches the fish.

**mercury** An element that occurs naturally in the environment and can accumulate in streams and oceans and in the bodies of fish.

**migration** The movement of fish from one place to another.

**overfishing** Depleting the population of a species by excessive (too much) fishing of it.

**pier** A walkway above a body of water.

**pollution** The presence of a substance or thing that has harmful or poisonous effects upon the surrounding environment and life-forms.

**scaling** Removing the scales from the skin of the fish.

**sinker** A weight used to sink a fishing line.

**steaking** Cutting the fish into steaks.

American Fisheries Society
5410 Grosvenor Lane
Bethesda, MD 20814
(301) 897-8616
Web site: http://www.fisheries.org
The mission of the American Fisheries Society is to improve the
conservation and sustainability of fishery resources and aquatic
ecosystems by advancing fisheries and aquatic science and pro-
moting the development of fisheries professionals.

Canadian Sportfishing Industry Association
1434 Chemong Road, Unit 11
Peterborough, ON K9J 6X2
Canada
(877) 822-8881
Web site: http://www.csia.ca
This association focuses on making sure Canadians have ample
recreational fishing opportunities and that fish populations are
managed to sustainable levels.

Environment Canada
Inquiry Centre
10 Wellington, 23rd Floor
Gatineau, QC K1A 0H3
Canada
(819) 997-2800
Web site: http://www.ec.gc.ca
Environment Canada works to protect the environment, conserve
the country's natural heritage, and provide weather and meteo-
rological information to keep Canadians informed and safe.

Monterey Bay Aquarium Seafood Watch
886 Cannery Row
Monterey, CA 93940
(831) 648-4800
Web site: http://www.montereybayaquarium.org
The Monterey Bay Aquarium Seafood Watch program helps
    consumers and businesses make good choices for healthy
    oceans. Their recommendations indicate which seafood items
    are best choices, good alternatives, and bad choices that
    people should avoid.

National Oceanic and Atmospheric Administration (NOAA)
NOAA Fisheries Service
1315 East West Highway
Silver Spring, MD 20910
Web site: http://www.nmfs.noaa.gov
NOAA's Fisheries Service is the federal agency responsible for the stew-
    ardship of the nation's living marine resources and their habitat. It is
    responsible for the management, conservation, and protection of
    living marine resources within the United States' Exclusive Economic
    Zone, which is water 3 to 200 miles (5–322 km) offshore.

U.S. Fish and Wildlife Service
1849 C Street NW
Washington, DC 20240
(800) 344-9453
Web site: http://www.fws.gov
The U.S. Fish and Wildlife Service works with others to conserve,
    protect, and enhance fish, wildlife, plants, and their habitats
    for the continuing benefit of the American people.

Wildlife Management Institute
1440 Upper Bermudian Road
Gardners, PA 17324
(717) 677-4480
Web site: http://www.wildlifemanagementinstitute.org
Founded in 1911, the Wildlife Management Institute is a private,
nonprofit, scientific, and educational organization dedicated to the
conservation, enhancement, and professional management of
North America's wildlife and other natural resources.

# Web Sites

Due to the changing nature of Internet links, Rosen Publishing has
developed an online list of Web sites related to the subject of this book.
This site is updated regularly. Please use this link to access the list:

http://www.rosenlinks.com/FISH/Pier

Benedetti, Marie. *Fishing with Grandpapa: The Most Important Rules.* Mustang, OK: Tate Publishing, 2008.

Boudreau, Helene. *Life in a Fishing Community* (Learn About Rural Life). New York, NY: Crabtree Publishing Company, 2009.

Bourne, Wade. *Basic Fishing: A Beginner's Guide.* New York, NY: Skyhorse Publishing, 2011.

Buzzacott, Francis H. *Lost Arts of the Sportsman: The Ultimate Guide to Hunting, Fishing, Trapping, and Camping.* New York, NY: Skyhorse Publishing, 2013.

Canfield, Jack. *Chicken Soup for the Fisherman's Soul: Fish Tales to Hook Your Spirit and Snag Your Funny Bone.* Cos Cob, CT: Chicken Soup for the Soul Publishing, 2012.

Carpenter, Tom. *Saltwater Fishing: Snapper, Mackerel, Bluefish, Tuna, and More.* Minneapolis, MN: Lerner, 2012.

Clove, Charles. *The End of the Line: How Overfishing Is Changing the World and What We Eat.* Berkeley, CA: University of California Press, 2008.

Gilbey, Henry. *Ultimate Fishing Adventures: 100 Extraordinary Fishing Experiences Around the World.* Chichester, England: Wiley Nautical, 2012.

Hilborn, Ray. *Overfishing: What Everyone Needs to Know.* New York, NY: Oxford University Press, 2012.

Howard, Melanie A. *Freshwater Fishing for Kids* (Into the Great Outdoors). North Mankato, MN: Capstone Press, 2012.

Kaminsky, Peter, and Greg Schwipps. *Fishing for Dummies.* Hoboken, NJ: For Dummies, 2011.

Kelley, K. C. *Let's Go Fishing* (DK Readers Boys' Life Series). New York, NY: DK Publishing, 2008.

McLimans, David. *Gone Fishing: Ocean Life by the Numbers.* London, England: Walker Childrens, 2008.

Paulsen, Gary. *Father Water, Mother Woods: Essays on Fishing and Hunting in the North Woods*. New York, NY: Bantam Doubleday Dell Books for Young Readers, 2012.

Pfeiffer, Boyd C. *The Complete Book of Rod Building and Tackle Making.* Guilford, CT: Lyons Press, 2013.

Philpott, Lindsey. *Complete Book of Fishing Knots, Lines, and Leaders*. New York, NY: Skyhorse Publishing, 2008.

Reed, Tom. *Blue Lines: A Fishing Life*. Helena, MT: Riverbend Publishing, 2010.

Safarik, Norman, and Allan Safarik. *Bluebacks and Silver Brights: A Lifetime in the BC Fisheries from Bounty to Plunder.* Toronto, ON, Canada: ECW Press, 2012.

Walker, Andrew. *How to Improve at Fishing.* New York, NY: Crabtree Publishing Company, 2009.

# BIBLIOGRAPHY

Bean, Tony. *The Last Smallmouth—The Definitive Smallmouth Bass Fishing Guide*. Martinsville, IN: Fideli Publishing, 2012.

Burdeau, Cain. "Two Years Later, Sick Fish Found Near BP Oil Spill Site." *USA Today*, April 19, 2012. Retrieved September 2012 (http://www.usatoday.com/money/economy/story/2012-04-19/bp-oil-spill-sick-fish-discovered/54415076/1).

Campfish.net. "Saltwater Fish." Retrieved September 2012 (http://campfish.net/saltwaterfish.php).

Dickie, J. L. *Forty Years of Trout and Salmon Fishing*. Charleston, SC: BiblioBazaar, 2009.

Ellison, Gene. *Teach Me Fishing: The Most Fun Ways to Teach Your Child Ages 3-13 How to Fish.* San Rafael, CA: Wonderdads, 2013.

FishingDestinGuide.com. "Fishing the Piers in the Destin Area." Retrieved September 2012 (http://fishingdestinguide.com/PIER-FISHING.html).

Forcier, Todd,."Fishing Safety Tips." LearningHowToFish.com. Retrieved September 2012 (http://www.learninghowtofish.com/pages/fishing-safety-tips.php).

Garden-Robinson, Julie, and Martin Marchello. "A Pocket Guide to Care and Handling of Fish from Stream to Table." North Dakota State University Extension Service, October 2003. Retrieved August 2012 (http://www.ag.ndsu.edu/pubs/yf/foods/fn535.pdf).

Holmes, Mike. *Fishing the Texas Gulf Coast: An Angler's Guide to More Than 100 Great Places to Fish.* Guilford, CT: Lyons Press, 2009.

Konway, Bill. "Extreme Aerial Bowfishing: Jumping Carp Breaks Woman's Jaw in Illinois." *Field and Stream*, August 21, 2009. Retrieved August 2012 (http://www.fieldandstream.com/photos/gallery/fishing/2009/08/when-carp-attack?photo=0#node-1001334939).

NationalGeographic.com. "Marine Pollution: Centuries of Abuse Have Taken a Heavy Toll." Retrieved September 2012 (http://ocean.nationalgeographic.com/ocean/critical-issues-marine-pollution).

NationalGeographic.com. "Overfishing: Plenty of Fish in the Sea? Not Always." Retrieved September 2012 (http://ocean.nationalgeographic.com/ocean/critical-issues-overfishing).

PierFishing.com. "Pier Fishing in California—Santa Cruz Wharf." Retrieved August 2012 (http://www.pierfishing.com/pier_of_the_month/santacruz.html).

Price, Steven D. *The Ultimate Fishing Guide*. New York, NY: HarperCollins, 1996.

Pumphrey, Clint. "Top 10 Most Endangered Fish Species." *Animal Planet*. Retrieved September 2012 (http://animal.discovery.com/adventure-fishing/sustainability/top-10-most-endangered-fish.html).

Solomon, Dane. *Fishing: Have Fun, Be Smart.* New York, NY: Rosen Publishing, 2000.

TakeMeFishing.org. "Take Me Fishing." Retrieved August 2012 (http://www.takemefishing.org/assets/downloads/when_to_fish.pdf).

Thompson, Tommy L. *The Saltwater Angler's Guide to Tampa Bay and Southwest Florida.* Gainesville, FL: University Press of Florida, 2012.

U.S. Food and Drug Administration. "Fresh and Frozen Seafood: Selecting and Serving It Safely." May 9, 2012. Retrieved September 2012 (http://www.fda.gov/food/resourcesforyou/consumers/ucm077331.htm).

Williams, Erik, and Malia Schwartz. "Catch-and-Release Fishing." Rhode Island Sea Grant Fact Sheet. Retrieved September 2012 (http://seagrant.gso.uri.edu/factsheets/catch-release_fs.html).

Withers, Cory. "Big Fish Makes Big News at Local Pier." *Topsail Advertiser*, August 25, 2010. Retrieved September 2012 (http://www.topsailadvertiser.com/articles/local-4857-big-person.html).

# INDEX

# About the Author

Mindy Mozer is a writer and editor living in Rochester, New York, with her husband and two children. She has written several books for Rosen on making the most of one's recreational, educational, and career opportunities.

# About the Consultant

Benjamin Cowan has more than twenty years of both freshwater and saltwater angling experience. In addition to being an avid outdoorsman, Cowan is a member of many conservation organizations. He currently resides in west Tennessee.

# Photo Credits

Cover, pp. 1, 3, 7, 11, 16, 23, 26, 32, 35, 37, 43, 51 © iStockphoto.com/ Joanna Pecha; pp. 4–5, 7, 11, 16, 23, 26, 32, 35, 37, 43, 51 (water) © iStockphoto.com/MichaelJay; p. 5 Lane V. Erickson/Shutterstock.com; p. 8 Jimmy Jacobs; p. 10 VisitStPeteClearwater.com; pp. 12, 17, 18–19, 21, 24–25, 40 Polly Dean; p. 14 Universal Images Group/Getty Images; p. 27 Shmuel Thaler; p. 29 Noel Hendrickson/ Photodisc/ Getty Images; p. 31 Vsevolodizotov/Shutterstock.com; p. 33 Will Salter/Lonely Planet Images/Getty Images; pp. 36, 41 iStockphoto/Thinkstock; p. 38 Teodor Ostojic/ Shutterstock.com; pp. 44–45 The Washington Post/Getty Images; p. 48 Barrett & MacKay/All Canada Photos/Getty Images; p. 50 Rich Carey/Shutterstock.com; p. 52 Image by Jack Scott/ Flickr/Getty Images; back cover and interior silhouettes (figures) © iStockphoto.com/A-Digit, Hemera/Thinkstock; back cover and interior silhouette (grass) © iStockphoto.com/Makhnach_M; back cover silhouette (hook) iStockphoto.com/Jason Derry.

Designer: Nicole Russo; Photo Researcher: Marty Levick